The Way the Crocodile Taught Me

For Melissa and Tim

The Way the Crocodile Taught Me

Katrina Naomi

Seren is the book imprint of
Poetry Wales Press Ltd.
57 Nolton Street, Bridgend, Wales, CF31 3AE
www.serenbooks.com
facebook.com/SerenBooks
twitter@SerenBooks

ISBN: 978-1-78172-331-9
ebook: 978-1-78172-332-6
Kindle: 978-1-78172-333-3

A CIP record for this title is available from the British Library.

The publisher acknowledges the financial assistance of the Welsh Books Council.

Cover image illustration by Gianna Pergamo. www.pergamopapergoods.com

Printed in Bembo by Bell & Bain Ltd, Glasgow.

Author Website: www.katrinanaomi.co.uk

Contents

I

II

III

I

2 Edinburgh Walk

A crazy pattern on the kitchen tiles,
each one scorched
with the curved ship of an iron,
its steam of holes oh oh ohing
on the orange glaze.

Mum frenzied with a brillo pad
at the former tenant's gift.
We lived with their jilted art
then looked on past
to the square of garden

where one day, Mum promised,
we'd have a swing.

Memory, (Margate 1969)

My father is muffled   he stands
away from my sister and I   We wear
identical hats   halos   of synthetic fur
tied with pom poms   He holds his new camera
The sun is low   level with my eyes
We stand on grass   just in front of the cliffs
He shouts in the wind   says it several times
Finally I understand   we are to smile
I stretch the muscles of my cheeks   they touch the fur
I don't know if my sister smiles   she is so far below me
He jokes about stepping back   I know I would die
I stay where I am   take my sister's small mitten in mine

The Romantic

After my father left, I grew
    a battery of hearts,
felt each of them beat,
    like doves in a casket

before their release. You might imagine
    the sheen of the good heart.
I rarely picture the razor wire heart,
    its zest and sting.

If I say my hearts have never been
    broken, or fissured, or ruptured,
that's not entirely true.
    Still, I want my faults intact.

And the barbs of the heart that loved my father jut
    as if from a pike's lower lip,
the war of rust leaking;
    a child's heart,
                no larger than a grenade.

My Parents' Poem

won't be set in couplets,
certainly won't rhyme.
I'll let you guess the refrain,
his envoi,
after a volley of verbs.
It will be Hughesian, Plathian,
well, from that era. It will be brief,
yet I won't understand it all.
A work of juvenilia,
their poem will try to marry certain ideals.
It will be written in the past tense
by another woman.

Yellow Dahlias

This is the image that sticks:
my married mother, her costume cut
low and high, one foot below

the impossible blue of a honeymoon pool,
the other poised on the metal step;
her face, fresh of make-up,

brows plucked in static surprise,
eyes wide with the rubber pull
of yellow dahlias, her new ring and bracelet.

A triumph. My mother emerging
from the water as I'd never seen her before.
Her head, a belisha beacon of hope.

Poems after my Step-father

1. Meeting my Fathers

Derek, first to arrive, is in Barbour shirt, sensible trousers;
Sonnie wears denims, shirt open to mid-chest,
his silver St Christopher hanging, heavy.
I don't know why I'm here. Derek has left
his collection of international friends in the saloon bar.
Sonnie unwraps his Toby jugs, sets them in a circle,
like an invocation –
then I remember, he's already dead.
My mother works behind the bar.
I pay for the drinks.
She looks at both men, can't decide between them,
can't imagine what she ever saw in either.
My sister wipes our table.
It's been so long, Derek doesn't recognise her,
wanders back to his friends.
Sonnie starts to disintegrate, becomes a slick,
something my mother will have to clear up.
I can probably sell the medallion.

2. The Fight Before my Sister's Wedding

never happened   Mum   Sonnie and Nan
Nan who wasn't there   all remember
nothing   The groom's Dad and Sonnie
my step-dad   didn't reach over the mock medieval sofa
didn't harden their faces   their fists
didn't swear or threaten   didn't reduce
my mum to tears   didn't crunch each other's cheeks
I never ducked between them   didn't dodge
punches   spittle   sweat   didn't push
the carefully distressed coffee table   its decanter of whisky
out of range   never got bruised   a grazed right arm
a cut left foot   never ushered the groom's father
and mother to the door   Sonnie didn't cry   begging me
to forgive him   I never said he was pathetic
never said I didn't want to be in the same room as him
ever again   If it wasn't for my foot wincing
on its white heel behind the fantasy of lace
I'd have believed my family   believed
I'd made it all up   just like before

3. Pop Socks and Manicures

Seeing the drag queens tonight, I wonder
if I've ever applauded you, and not known.

Your wardrobe was always locked.
I'd got used to your kimono, pop socks and manicures,

hair dye, eyelash tint, the annual trip to Thailand.
I wouldn't have cared about a rack of dresses

several sizes larger than hers, your huge stilettos.
I wasn't that sort of child. I'm still not.

I scan the faces of these men. Perhaps, one night,
we won't argue, we'll sing. Just sing.

4. Portrait of my Step-father as a Xmas Tree

Your bulk visible through the front door's fake frosted panes;
your too many arms, ecstatic at such a public display of glitz,

at what you usually only donned when you were alone;
your lights flashing danger off and on; your moods impossible

to extinguish. I could never pass without your daily demand
that the house be hoovered before I could run to school;

your piney smell felled by an insistence of Kouros, reaching out
past your meretricious shine and cheer. Yet unlike a Xmas tree,

you weren't so easy to dislodge; there would be no pale forest
of step-fathers littering the street. You were in our house for keeps.

5. Willpower

He couldn't say no to a fried egg sarnie, smeared with Daddies sauce,
eating two as a snack. Other days, our step-father barely ate,
yet was up at 4, his engine running, as he lifted truckloads of turf.
He was always jumpy, mostly in a temper in our front room,
we were all hemmed in by the giant sofa. When he didn't eat,
he was worse; resenting the lack of food, his 17 stones, me,
the eldest, who ate what she wanted and stayed slim.
And he couldn't eat or sleep after work, but sprawled on the couch
in silk pyjama bottoms, lolloping breasts bared as he flicked
between channels, riffled through *The Sport* and *The People*.
He bought his slimming tablets – whizz, amphetamines, speed –
in bulk in Thailand. Gave my sister two when she said she'd put on weight.
She skipped breakfast, lunch and tea, her brown eyes buzzed
through school, her heart sprinted for days. She learnt to say no
to his pills, his fried egg sarnies. His moods darkened,
though he never hit us like he did our mother.
I once told him to punch me and his ice blue eyes screwed into mine,
acid in the crease of his lips, his florid face too close;
then he'd catch the tv's whine of motor racing and heave his frame
back to the sofa and I'd escape, another drug bolting through my veins –
sometimes hate, sometimes pity, but always cut with fear.

6. Step-father Graph

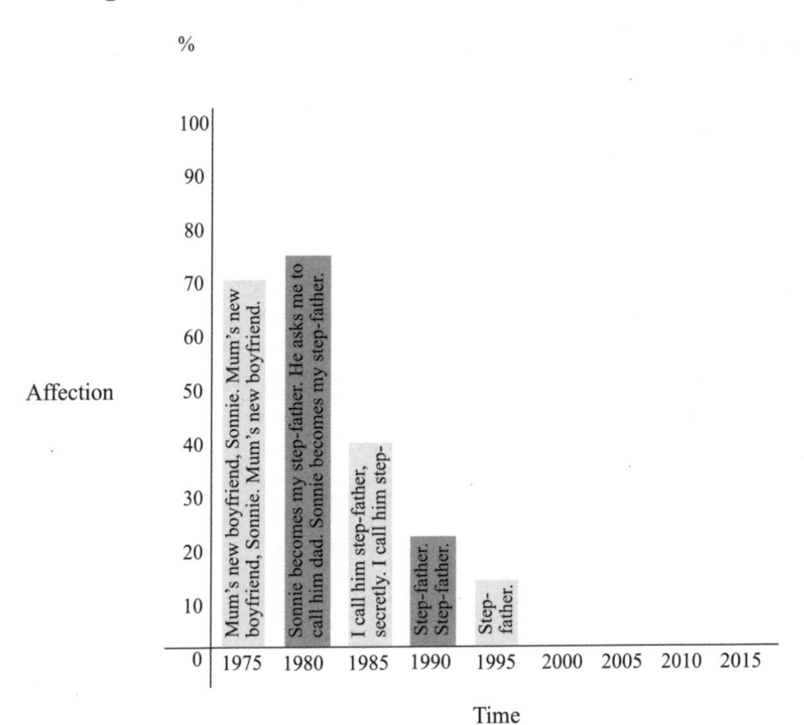

7. Self-portrait with Top Hat

I parade with this symbol of male power,
of weddings, of funerals, wedged on my crown.
Finally my step-father has died.
I practise putting on, taking off this news,
these heavy layers before the mirror. I shoot
photos of myself in full mourner's attire, the top
of this top hat, its whirl of black rabbit,
just out of the frame. Today, I'm cross-
dressing in memory of him. I could pass
with my mascara'd moustache, hair
piled into the dark, and I sway, silver-tipped cane
my constant companion; a mean dancer
as I place this topper in its box. I'm glad
the funeral's over, that he's also in his box.

Leopard Print Coat

I love the coat's fakery,
the brash barmaid ballsiness of it,
each fibre thrilling to the musk and cloy
of my mother's Youth Dew.

I've still not had it cleaned;
my neck's grease mingles with hers,
my small breasts flatten into the space
hers once made.

I'd never have worn this coat
had my sister not stolen up
the flock-walled stairs.
He didn't know she had a key.

He never saw me wear it.
Never.

And this coat dreams of glitterballs,
of cider *and* Pomagne,
of gold crochet catsuits,
of sashaying down the Old Kent Road.

Whistle

The sea's so far out I glimpse Margate's harbour lights.
Cormorants elbow

as if something might happen beside a shift
in the tide. I wade

with my sister. The bay tastes our skin; salt hangs
heavy round our thighs.

The doll's house, our hut on the prom, distant.
I hear Mum's call

– her two-fingered, three-note whistle –
travel from that world to this.

The Red Room

Like a murder – my mother's kitchen items rinsed with blood.
Borrowed blood, pumped out, donated, transfused so many times.
Her anniversary: six years on, things seem cheerier than they might,
because I know what happened. There was no killing, it was humane –
like the slaughter of a sheep is humane.

I can look in this room now, like I might see with a tiny camera into my intestines.
All is still, though I'm told every organ is in working order.
Her heart isn't in this room. She's taken it to that other place.

Chunks of her dyed, titian hair remain in a carmine suitcase,
her scarlet nail clippings moon in a crimson dish,
her vixen leather mini skirt grins from a rusting hook.

I hope her new room has many colours.
I plant a bulb of amaryllis.

Letter to my Mother

You lie underneath him,
a measure of mud between you.

This was our final argument – his and mine –
your husband/my step-father.

I'm told of a double headstone,
which I haven't visited,

since I held my niece's hand,
threw a lily and a tablespoon of chalky soil

on your lid. I can't talk to you,
knowing he's also there, listening,

as he always did: the click
of the extension by your bed, the reading

out of my letters and your replies.
All these years, his 17 stones

pressing down on you, crushing
the soil between you.

I talk to you when I cross the Thames,
looking right to Shooters Hill –

Kent's north edge. I send you my words
in a flotilla of paper boats. I forgive you,

as I always have. I forgive you
for marrying him.

Boredom: An Appreciation

The heavy-shouldered clock of morning,
those slender hands never reaching
past the hours of brown wallpaper.

I don't have time for boredom now,
to stare at the gas in the fire,
as if I could study flames,

to let my thoughts drift on their thermal,
unharnessed, as if they were never mine –
never could be.

Might I long for a Westgate afternoon,
waiting for the yellow lights
of evening, knowing day had melted –

the dark toffee of it – to listen
to the hiss, the end of the cassette,
re-reading my diary, its brief entries.

And if I sit here long enough,
could I wonder where that jet goes
with its teatime, pinkish trail,

imagine being a passenger,
the tedium of that life,
while I bite the ends of my hair.

Poems after my Nan

1. Family Dentist

Nan taught me to knot a milk tooth to a handle
then slam the door. Her trick worked –
out it came – though the gloss paint suffered.

I was said to have her knack with wobbly teeth,
rocking each baby on a stub of fresh enamel,
claiming the bubble of blood, its oily sheen.

Nothing fossilised in our jellied gums.
If my sister didn't fancy the door and handle,
I grasped her tooth and twisted the root.

Years later, Nan spoke of her visit to the dentist:
every molar, wisdom and incisor
removed – a present for her twenty-first.

2. Two Aprons

after Arshile Gorky

I have my limitations, I can only paint.
Each silver tube has its own sound,
its own idea of life and how it might be lived.

Here's the yellow of Nan's Portuguese pinny,
I heard its cockcrow from the drawer –
and me, not even of the generation that wears aprons,

though I'm wearing one now, its white cottons
unravelling like the lines of this painting.

I release the bird from the stuffy drawer,
its wattle and plumage crushed,
yet the colours still sing to the morning.

While I search for clues to Nan's journeys,
her many tongues jumble in my apron's pockets,
and this cockerel will star on the canvas.

3. What Nan Said

On my first trip home from college:
You've got ideas above your station.

As if I should've stayed below stairs,
never ventured out of our sitcom.

I'd probably been showing off –
talking politics in French.

Nan didn't get to study:
Some of us had to work for a living.

I can translate all of this
now I've travelled above ground.

If Nan were here, I'd try to tell her
I'm still the same girl, la même.

4. Her Advice After my Partner's Breakdown

What did you know of love?
You, who slept in a separate bed,
separate room, who knew nothing of us.

You told me to let him be,
let him get on with it, let him alone.
You gave me your harshest advice,

told me what you'd done
after Grandpa was discharged from the Navy;
hiding from the merest sound, from you.

You made me hear every whistle
and blast of your advice.
And I never thanked you.

5. Gin and Ice Cream

Even after all the gins, all morning,
you still can't say the c-word.

Over a weekend, I try to discuss your daughter/
my mum, but your soft blue eyes fill.

You ask me to water the roses,
stabbing at the crust of a lemon cheesecake,

scooping out the last of the ice cream.
The petals drip. We won't talk of this again.

When Mum comes round you hug her so tight
to the mismatched buttons of your pink housecoat,

the air stills. We watch her, like royalty,
searching her eyes, her movements.

We smile hard, draining and weighing
each of her words:

oedema, tamoxifen, oncologist.
Her stay, as always, is brief.

After she leaves, I raise a silent toast
and together, we finish the bottle.

6. The Woman on the Sideboard

It was you, 40 years back,
an over-the-shoulder glance.
You don't know yourself
or me, anymore.

After I helped sort your earrings,
you said how the Lord Mayor
had come to find your butterflies,
match pearls with pearls, enamel with enamel.

I've had to say goodbye to your lamb stews,
Singer sewing machine, photos of Sorrento.
They've all gone into storage;
you keep wrenching the hinge.

You're still my nan,
even if I'm your mayor.

7. Another Planet

She's leaving this planet,
her roses neglected for spanners, bolts.
I hadn't read the signs, didn't know
she'd been working on that rocket.
And it's complete. I can't think
why I didn't notice this before. I see now
she's packed a small leather case.
So few items. I know very little
about this new earth, if there's a moon,
a sun, lakes, a tide. She's changing
into her silk dress and jacket,
plumping her hair. She doesn't look back,
just shoulders into her coat.
The kitchen door hovers in the artificial breeze.
She's left me everything.

8. Elsie

I want them to let me go. I didn't ask
for their fancy stitching dissolving in my leg;
the yellow and the black, the green and the blue.
I didn't ask them to open up my hip, to peer in,
like they have the right. I'll attack again,
if they come with their tubes, their needles,
their armband of air, somebody's leftover blood.
They've taken my teeth; I can still spit
and scratch. I've ripped out their saline drip,
made a mess of my wrist, gutted my side seam.

This is my life. My death. I could eat
their cake, their shepherd's pie, their trifle.
I could drink their half-cold tea in the baby's beaker,
could grow into my folds of skin.
Instead, I yank their nightie up to my neck –
breasts larger than a pair of implants.
I've frightened my granddaughters,
squeezed their hands until they've cried.
I want them to let me go –
to go out in a blaze of Elsie.

9. Full Strength

I love someone I no longer know.
And I'm waiting to feel the full strength
of that love. She's stopped eating, drinking,
she's bringing it on.
                                        Staring into her silent howl,
that dark oval beneath cheekbones that hurt,
I wonder what words she might form
in the space where words no longer come.

She remains with her animal nature –
an animal in distress – and for a moment,
I consider whether it would be just
to pick up her pillow.
                                        My sister and I
have chosen Sinatra, pink roses
on wicker, a sherry reception at The Swan –
all possibly what she'd have wanted.

At my Sister's

I carefully pick elderberries
from the blue-fleece soles
of these borrowed slippers;

focus on a wide screen of washing,
how the orange of my cardy on the line
argues with a red admiral on a bleached out towel.

The washing machine yawns itself alive;
the radiator, the dishwasher, all sing
their siren songs to usefulness.

The steady hum shifts me to the hospital.
My sister visits her husband.
A dog barks at the flapping of next door's union jack.

I try my quiet, a turning of pages,
but the house draws me back
to the bickering cycle of family life.

This is the end of the season:
a place of falling apples, of wonky aerials,
all obeying the same master in their slippage,

like a thorn bush on a moor.

II

The Woman who Married the Berlin Wall

fell in love at the age of seven, thrilling
to this Berliner's slim sensuality,
his horizontal lines, his sense of division;
found the Great Wall of China *far too stout.*

She used the words *he* or *my husband*,
made models of her lover, took him on sleigh rides
so he could enjoy her native northern Sweden.

She papered her rooms from bulging scrapbooks.
On her sixth visit, they wed: a small ceremony.
She scratched her desire deep into his core;
knowing he couldn't leave until he was demolished,
chunk by chunk. She felt she owned him outright.

I have some sympathy for a woman who could love a wall.
I have practised kissing tables, licking car seats,
have pressed myself against an aeroplane's wing.

Bearskin

I like noughts and crosses   hangman
played a lot of that with the kids
makes me a bit nostalgic   You don't mind?
Only I don't see them anymore
I still think of them   as kids
still   they're grown up now
probably got kids of their own
I get a card from my eldest at Xmas
it cracks me up   seeing her
handwriting   I blame the wife   don't remember
hitting her   I joined that fathers' group
clambered about on rooftops   a bit undignified
for a soldier   I've calmed down now   Needed to
I used to travel   a lot   Too much
Got up to some things I shouldn't of
specially for a soldier   Word got around
In '98 or maybe '97   I passed out on parade
dropped my gun   Everyone was kind
For a while   I really tried   You believe me?
And then   there was the drink   Still is
I'm not boring you?   Only I miss my mates
in the guard   miss my kids   miss Janey
Did I tell you I had to go away for a bit?
I used to love that bearskin

Breakfast at the New Hampshire Motel

The only woman, I carry a crushable glass
of sweetened orange juice, fortified
with Vitamin C, and a polystyrene cup
of the weakest, lukewarm coffee. The table
offers fake freesias, an overstuffed chair
upholstered with plastic. I watch
a thin man in black and Cuban heels
stride to his Harley. While the truckers
are softly spoken, their tattoos yell
above cut-off vests and Caterpillar boots.
No one says good morning. All of them try
not to stare. And I try not to squirm
on the squeaky seat at the tv sitcom,
at the advert for vaginal deodorant.

The Bicycle

I was OK   nothing had happened
nothing bad had happened
I couldn't get up from the bench
couldn't do up my dungarees
It was cold   it was night
The man had gone   and that was good
I was OK   I could sit up
peel myself from the bench's slats
which had pressed deep inside
It could have been worse
I was shaking   it was night
The bicycle was too heavy
My dungarees kept slipping
buttons were missing
I had to get home
It was so hard to walk
My head hurt   kept punching inside
my teeth couldn't stop talking
It could have been worse
My jaw hurt and my breasts were raw
I couldn't pick up the bicycle   its spinning wheel
couldn't walk with the bicycle
I had to get home   to wash
sleep   throw these clothes away
I was shaking   I was cold
My dungarees wouldn't do up
I would be alright   it was just
this bicycle   I needed

On the Shore

Walking from Anstruther to Crail,
        no beach to speak of, and I can't be sure
if the cries come from my mouth or the oystercatcher's throat.
        Land continues its slide to the sea, splashes of plastic,
jags of rock angle into rain and a plover's curve.

BEWARE LIVESTOCK. A pig and I consider
        each other, and I wonder – not for the first time –
if I could cut into such an animal, take her life, as we hold
        our breath, eye to eye, either side of a buzzing wire.
She returns to her young, teats bared like teeth.

In the distance, a house tight to the shore, its roof
        lifted clean away. I think of a woman who gutted fish,
brushed her hair one hundred times a night, made love,
        her cries carried off by the birds. Here and there,
clumps of her voice remain, bright as daffodils.

Fledgling

A corner of your room's lined with the stuffing from pillows,
pieces of speckled shell. I've seen you perch on the ledge,
half-out, half-in, not knowing whether you'll jump or soar.

I think of those men who strapped on heavy plumage,
stood on cliffs and faced the breeze; those scientists
who studied the dinosaur of feathers. You're still waiting

for your scratchy wings to sprout, for your fall to earth
to be spectacular, your legs greeting the ground, travelling
up through your pelvis and into your guts. And I think

of Amelia Earhart, who knew just how much to believe
in herself. You sit in the cold air, a boy and the moon,
calling to your new friends, safe in their branches,

as you test your language, fashioning yourself after a finch.
Your eyes glitter; a dish of worms writhe at your side.
In the morning, I'll unravel the strings of my kite.

Bestial

after Moniza Alvi

My husband took to running on all fours,
sniffed me to communicate, licked and nuzzled.
For my birthday, he fetched peonies from the park,
snapped at the roots in his teeth.
He liked his arse in the air,
balls swinging like a lion's in their hairy nest.
His shoulder blades triangled, winged,
as if he might leave rectangular contact with earth,
become a little Pegasus.
Instead, he upped his mileage –
four legs good, he'd quote at marathon officials.
On our first anniversary, to prove my love (and to help his posture),
I took him to the optician who made him spectacles
with upward reflecting mirrors to keep his spine in line with his neck –
he ran all the faster.
One night, he asked to be excused from the table,
lapped his food from a silver dish at my feet,
slept at the foot of the bed.
Sex was barely any different to before
but I had to lower myself for his kisses.
I baulked at his pleading for a collar and lead.
Initially.

Concrete Overcoat

I was told Ronnie and Reggie used to start
at the feet and work their way up,
bulges rising in their matching trousers,

that they took such care not to splash
their suits, their matt black shoes,
as they mixed and shovelled, as they thundered

wet stones and sand over ankles, legs and chest,
arms and neck. I was told how their victim's
pleas were drowned by a larger mouth,

its heavy tongue slopping round and round,
while the twins sculpted the man's hair
(grey overnight) to a perfect quiff –

just like Ronnie's. Was told how they set
each eye, the colour of steel, how they funnelled
liquid concrete, the steady porridge of it,

into a throat: like an Aztec pouring
molten gold down a gullet;
a farmer force-feeding a duck.

The Way the Crocodile Taught Me

I swooned at the large god of him, sunning.
A tooth for every day of my life.
He performed his run along the bank,
as males do. I brought my boat closer.
He took to following, at a distance.

I wasn't taken in, knew his four-chambered heart
pumped love out and in, in and out,
knew his tongue had few good uses,
knew all about his grin. Yet whoever said he was cold-
blooded has never truly known this beast.

He brought out the prehistoric in me. I dived.
We swam, belly to belly, to where the Niles meet,
tussled as we thrashed among the weeds. After, I lay
the length of him, a limestone lilo, studs patterning
my skin. He smiled at me, often. Taught me all he knew.

Years later, when a man tried to drag me under,
I practised the force my lover had held back –
levered my small jaws open to their furthest extent,
splashed them down on the human's arm.
My attacker still carries the mark of my smile.

September

This is unknown;
my bright, berry blood comes late,
follows a new calendar.

Soon, I'll say goodbye
to this belching red,
this faint anaemia, goodbye

to the children
I never wanted. Last night,
walking back from the village,

I saw them in the waning moon,
holding hands, running
away from me.

We are All Saying Nothing

                and we're saying it
with silence   with murmurs
of paint   of absence
                                of music
people   colour   And I'm saying
nothing of those people
            do you hear me?
                                     Here
the rage of the quiet voice
she who joins in   even if
no one listens
                        absent
                                Hush
            She used to
collaborate   saying nothing
saying it again
                          So much space
between the loud
                             between colours
more than she can say
and she's not saying it
                                   she's not
In the absence
of colour   in the scrape of it
              Quiet
                          in the grey echo
behind colour   in the ambient
              a small voice   quiet   at first

And Mandy Talks of Kyrgyzstan

I focus on the yellow of tulips
the mauve of bluebells,
their woodscent over bitter-
sweet coffee, the sun on next door's wall.
The world washes in, the froth
of my life drains its circular swing
down the basin's neat holes.

Central Asia's politics had swirled away
from me – its gas, its oil – I'd forgotten
everything: the government shooting,
the 200 dead. Here, I could slip
back in, like a swimmer,
break the film of my bubble,
have the tin of words sink.

I focus on the points of tulips
– all speaking at once –
their water slowly running out.

Wolf on a Hillside

There were two of you, unless a man shouts and answers himself,
like a brother's echo across a loch. You brought the place alive, prowling
round their cabins before dawn, alive to how it could *feel*, listening
to their breathing, their muffled snores. Could you imagine with your torch
what each wore under the duvet? Had you seen both women lit up, alone
in their cabins, high above the cedars – a brilliant invitation?
And which would you have preferred, the taller, the shorter,
the blonder, the darker? Perhaps you talked of swapping at a set half-time,
say 5 am, taking the other, giving each marks out of 10? Would you have left them
alive or barely? Did you curse your girth, unable to slink
through the skylight the tall one had thoughtfully left open?
Did you feel like a wolf on a hillside? Did you want them awake,
to chase through the sweet-smelling cabins, was that part of the game?
You tried every key in your pocket, pawed at bolts and windows.
You huffed and puffed at their houses, hurring the reinforced glass.
The locks, the windows, the timber held. You clomped away in your steel-
capped boots, turned the music up in your car, as if this was some recompense.

Comfort Me with Apples

Beware their shiny cheeks;
the curl of peel spelling out her name.

Beware their bite;
the taste of flesh, the sweetness of her breath.

Build me towers of every kind of apple,
lock the harvest away.

Beware the sun,
for I can only countenance night.

Bid me drink from rotten fruits
whose juice has turned to spirit –

only then shall you comfort me with apples,
for I am sick of love.

The History Teacher

knew he'd made a mistake; should never have retrained.
He smiled through a yawn of discussion on today's wars;
give him trenches, the Crimea, the blood of the Middle Ages.
He'd argued for the introduction of the Inquisition
into the curriculum. Sensed Year 5 were ready
for the careful splinter of a finger, the scraping out of an eye,
flaying, the separation of joint and muscle.
During exams, he found himself walking the rows of heads,
admiring the beef of a shoulder, the heft of a plump hip.
This took him back to the Rorschach of splattered aprons
as he folded them up at the end of the day.
He'd followed his father into butchery, understood
it wasn't done to swing the cleaver so high, to relish
hacking at a spinal cord. And he pictured himself, naked
to the waist but for a rough hood, removing Charles I's wig,
guiding the quivering neck on to the rounded block.
But here he was sneezing in chalk dust,
expected to lecture on social history, and all he could think of
was the delicacy of lifting a chicken's wing,
before the thud when you hit it, dead right,
and the bird fell apart. He didn't feel safe
with kids – their animation – hated the way he imagined them,
and himself: making his choice of knives,
stroking the freezer's long arm. He'd been in the wrong trade
even then. It was the saws of the abattoir that called him.
He reminisced about the mornings he'd wandered past
the open door, its plastic strips smeared and glued,
how he'd peered in through the buzz of flies.
At first, the men laughed at his cap and shorts, yet gradually
welcomed him, and he'd stroll in the artificial light
among the twitching cows, their plumes of breath,
grin as the men 'forgot' the stun. Out came the machines,
shearing through the toenail yellow of fat.
He'd asked to slice a vein, watched the spurt through half-closed eyes,
until it hung like paint on the hosedown wall and he gulped in
the smell as if he were drinking. And here he was,
facing a class of dumb animals, ones he couldn't even touch,
let alone show the glint of a blade.

for Clive

The Bear

One night, a waltz crept through my shutters,
    I followed the string of moons, placed the bear's palm
in my right, pressed my cheek to his stinking chest.

I used to long for our bearwalk, to drop a krone
    in a tin to keep the beast alive. Father ushered me past
the iron hoop of nostrils, past the rattling bracelets.

The keeper squeezed a jig from a painted box,
    the bear rose hind-leg tall, chains dancing in the off-beat,
before he sank back into the mystery of himself.

The Woman Who Walks Naked

sweeps her hair into a bun, soon she'll lop it off, anything to feel
that burn on her neck – the sun's gentle strangle.

She crosses the yard, her shadow tight, clangs the roasting gate,
forces her legs through the soup of midday – the heat glad
to get hold of her shoulders, the greasy sway of her breasts.

Nobody's in the field, the lane, the square. She scoops an armful
from the fountain over her back for the sun to sting dry.
Village dogs scoot towards her, sniffing her shins.
It's when she passes the café that the shout goes up.

III

Mantra

Staring into the golden eyes of Buddha, I wanted to believe.
On the trek to the foothills, I queued at the entrance to a cave,
handed over 200 rupees to the 80-year-old lama in red robes,
amber beads, a Smurf hat. I was curious about isolation,
how someone could live so far from people. Yet here we were,
12 of us, along with his wife who grew spinach in the lower hills
and checked our money. The lama smiled more than the nuns,
more than any of our priests. He had to angle his chin
to look into my face. I ignored the hint of flirtation,
wanted to believe this glint was enlightenment; remembered
my first holy communion and for an instant, I forgot about the cold,
the money, my blisters, the rest of the group.
I summoned a space,
to take what I could (though Mum would've questioned
why the lama hadn't washed his robes – I'd have explained
about the luxury of water up here; she'd have frowned
her 'no excuse for dirt' look) as the lama knotted a mantra
into a cord, stood on tiptoe, raised his arms and placed the cord
around my neck: a mini garland, a bootlace tie of red and yellow.
I knew it was mass produced, imagined devotees (or his wife)
lumbering a bale of it up to the cave, as the old man muttered.
I meant to ask about the colours, but thought again of my mum,
not long dead.
I took the blessing for her. In her last few years,
she'd asked me to light candles, knowing I didn't believe.
I'd entered churches, heard the coins drop into the silence
of a black box, watched the fake flames twitch below a gaudy saint,
just in case this act could make a difference. And I thought again,
how even in death, she was buried below that man she'd come to hate –
a man who'd begun building her a rockery, taking her to dinner,
and ended up telling her what she could and couldn't wear,
what colour to dye her hair, when she could take the dog for a walk
(and for how long), what she could eat, who she could speak to;
who'd read her letters before she did, who'd married her and hit her
I don't know how many times, she wouldn't say.
Her first husband
went off with another woman, who didn't have children, didn't live
in a council house, didn't have to save to pay the gas bill in a red tin box,
hearing the coins fall, the box shaken and weighed each week.

Yes, I took the blessing for her, raped at the age of 17, who'd told no one
apart from her husbands (who'd used this knowledge against her).
And then she'd told me, just before she died.
                                                                              I took what the lama offered,
Mum would've liked the ritual, the incense, the views. I wore the cord
with its simple knot, like a vow, until we reached the pass at Thorong-La
five days later, the highest I'll ever walk. I burrowed beneath my layers,
lifted the cord from my neck, looped it to a rope of prayer flags, with a knot
a mariner might approve of. I left it whipping in the Annapurna winds,
way above the snow.
                                                It was safe to cry then, at having come that far –
the closest I'd get to her, again. Later, I followed the scree path down,
lungs and brain gulping at oxygen, down to sweet ginger tea. Mum stayed,
repeating her mantra to the mountains, for six months, maybe a year,
before the cord unravelled, and then she'd be free.

Acknowledgements

With thanks to the editors of: *The TLS*; *The Poetry Review*; *The Spectator*; *New Welsh Review*; *The Dark Horse*; *Irish Literary Review*; *The London Magazine*; *The Lampeter Review*; *The Rialto; Magma; Ambit; The SHOp; Smiths Knoll; Stand; The Reader; Yellow Nib; Popshot; Ink, Sweat & Tears; Acumen; Prole; Glits-e; Poetry Society* website.

'Bearskin', 'Fledgling' and 'The Way the Crocodile Taught Me' were written during 'The Argument: Art V. Poetry', a collaborative project with the artist Tim Ridley, and first exhibited at the Poetry Café in London and the StAnza Poetry Festival in Scotland.

'The Bear' won second prize in the 2012 Poetry on the Lake Competition (short poem category) and 'The Woman Who Walks Naked' was highly commended.

'September' was commended in the 2011 Poetry Society Stanza Competition.

'Comfort Me with Apples' was commissioned by Poetry Wivenhoe and first published in *KJV – Old Text, New Poems* (Poetry Wivenhoe), 2011. The poem uses two phrases from the KJV bible.

A version of 'Another Planet' was first published in *Lunch at the Elephant & Castle* (Templar Poetry), 2008.

Thanks to Anne Welsh for allowing me to use a line of hers in my poem 'Two Aprons'.

Thanks to Judy Brown and to my supervisors at Goldsmiths, Stephen Knight and Blake Morrison, for their comments on this manuscript, and to Amy Wack and the team at Seren.

Finally, I would like to thank the Royal Literary Fund for a grant to enable me to complete this collection.